THIS BOOK IS NOT ABOUT STUDY SKILLS.

IT'S ABOUT GETTING A GOOD JOB AFTER YOU GRADUATE.

The #1 reason most students give for attending college is "to get a good job."

The skills outlined in *Making Your Mark* will help you graduate from college. But more important, these skills will see you through your entire career. It's kind of like a 2-for-1 deal. The college success skills you develop are the same employment skills you'll need for your career: good work habits, efficient time management, and an organized system for getting your work done at a high standard. If you approach your college years as professional development for your career, you'll be well prepared for the workplace, and you'll come as close as it gets to guaranteeing yourself a good job upon graduation.

LDF Publishing Inc.
1881 Yonge Street
P.O. Box 48086
Toronto, ON M4S 3C6

T. 416.484.8118 / 1.877.492.6845
F. 416.484.8118

info@makingyourmark.com
www.makingyourmark.com

LISA FRASER
9TH EDITION

MAKING YOUR MARK

DEVELOP THE MOTIVATION AND SKILLS TO ACHIEVE HIGH-PERFORMANCE COLLEGE AND CAREER SUCCESS

LDF Publishing Inc.

Making Your Mark
9th Edition
Lisa Fraser
ISBN 978-0-9735298-3-8

Publishing and Purchasing Information
Making Your Mark can be purchased at special volume discounts.
It is also available in French: *Comment réussir dans ses études*

LDF Publishing Inc.
1881 Yonge Street
P.O. Box 48086,
Toronto, ON M4S 3C6

T. 416.484.8118 / 1.877.492.6845
F. 416.484.8118

info@makingyourmark.com
www.makingyourmark.com

Cover and interior design by Dylan Royal
www.dylanroyal.com

"WE ARE W
REPEATED
EXCELLEN
IS NOT AN
A HABIT."

HAT WE

LY DO.

CE, THEN,

ACT, BUT

— Aristotle

01 HIGH-PERFORMANCE COLLEGE AND CAREER SUCCESS

This book is designed to help you get through college and, more important, to help you get the most out of college. Whether you are a

- first-year student,
- returning student,
- student athlete,
- nontraditional student who hasn't been in the classroom in years, or a
- high school student preparing for college,

you probably have a common goal: to graduate with the best academic performance possible, having spent the least amount of time studying.

We believe that by using your time well and by studying as efficiently as possible, you'll get more out of your education, and you'll have more time for life outside the classroom.

We've included the success tools that have proven most beneficial to students in the past, but after you've taken a look through them, you can decide which ones will work for you. As you read through this book, we'd like you to keep one thing in mind: the skills that will make you successful in college are the same skills that will make you successful in the workplace. In fact, we don't even use the term "study skills" —we prefer to call them "career success skills." We've found that students excel when they perceive and develop college success skills as if they're career skills.

Building an Educational and Career Vision

A large part of your college success will depend on how comfortable you are with the program you've selected. You'll have a much better chance of succeeding if you're sure you're in the right place and if you view your college years as professional development for your career. This mindset can help you get through courses you may not initially see as useful, but in the big picture, will help you achieve the greater goal of developing a lifelong career.

Have I Made the Right Choice?

You may be enrolled in a program that leads to a specific career, or you might be taking an undeclared or a transfer program. Either way, it's likely that you've experienced some degree of uncertainty about your career or program choice. It's common to have doubts and second thoughts, and the pressure to make "the perfect decision" can feel monumental.

Before you spend too much time worrying about your future, though, consider the following: rather than trying to make a final decision right now, you could approach your career as something that doesn't have to be fully defined at this time. It may be reassuring to know that most people don't have ultimate clarity about their careers. In fact, many of those out in the workforce still think about alternative career paths and opportunities. There is no perfect or final decision. Careers are always evolving, and it's a rare person who has only one career in his or her lifetime.

What's important is to continually add to your skill base so that you're always prepared for change. People who stay current with trends in the workplace are better able to find employment in any economic climate. Keep in mind that it isn't the career you choose that matters—no decision is irreversible or binding—it's the work ethic and attitude you display that will determine your success. If you decide to change your career path, you can always pick up the necessary industry skills if you're willing to invest the time.

So don't sweat it if you haven't resolved the career issue. If you're lucky enough to be sure of what you want to do, that's terrific. If you're still undecided, there's lots of time to figure it all out. Either way, focus on developing the one thing that's certain you'll need throughout your life: career success skills, which are transferable to any profession.

Me Inc and the 8 Cornerstones of High Performance

According to the U.S. Bureau of Labor, the median number of years that an employee stays with an employer ranges from 3.4 to 3.8 years. So again, whether you know your career direction or whether you're undeclared, what's constant is the need to develop a complete set of employability skills that will see you through any number of career changes.

We like the concept of Me Inc: be your own company and develop the best all-round set of career skills you can. Then no matter what happens, you'll have your Me Inc skill set to take with you wherever you go.

The first step in developing your skill set is adopting a career success mindset: thinking of your education as career development versus a program load made up of courses, grades, syllabi, and texts.

Exercise

1.1

Characteristics of a High-Performance Career

An important part of developing a career plan is understanding the difference between a job and a career so you'll know the range of the skills required to reach your career goal. In the spaces below, list five characteristics of a minimum wage job and five characteristics of a high-performance career.

Characteristics of a Minimum Wage Job   **Characteristics of a Career**

1. ....   1. ....

2. ....   2. ....

3. ....   3 ....

4. ....   4. ....

5. ....   5. ....

To help create a clear vision of where your education is leading you and what you're working toward, we make a distinction between a career and a job.

In this context, a career is a high-performance job that requires postsecondary schooling and has the potential for advancement and a high economic salary, among other things. The preparation for a career requires a long-term commitment and strategy; you can go out right now and get a minimum wage job, but it takes a considerable investment to develop a career.

Additional ways a career differs from a job:

You build a career over time and continue to develop it over a lifetime. A career has unlimited potential—both financial and developmental—if you're willing to continuously learn and grow within your industry. While a career requires a sizeable investment of time and effort, the payback is considerable: you like what you do, the financial reward is greater, and you have more control over your work life in terms of the hours you work, when you work them, and how much you get paid for them.

On the other hand, the required skills for a minimum wage job can be learned in the workplace within a set training period. A job doesn't usually have the same opportunities for advancement, transferability, or financial growth—there are often limits to how far you can go, how much you make, the hours you work, and when you work them.

Me Inc Mindset

A Me Inc career plan includes a high-performance approach to both college and your career. We encourage you to adopt a mindset that's based on the continual development of yourself as a complete package of valuable skills that will see you through your entire career. The high-performance skills outlined in Me Inc and the 8 Cornerstones of High Performance are the backbone of any career and are the lifelong skills that will help you be successful throughout college and your career.

Exercise

1.2

The Million $$$ Motivator

Compare minimum wage for a lifetime with a high-performance career wage.

The 8 Cornerstones of Me Inc are the difference between a lower-paying job and a high-performance salary. Don't get us wrong—we have the greatest respect for minimum wage jobs. Many of our most valuable skills and experiences come from minimum wage jobs, and these jobs are an integral part of our economy and society. However, because you have the opportunity to become a high-performance wage earner, we'd like to show you the lifetime difference between the two salaries, which may help you decide whether working toward this goal is for you.

1. Calculate minimum wage for a lifetime:

$.......... /hr × 40 hrs/wk = $................

× 50 wks/year =............................

× 40 yrs = $.............................

2. Calculate a high-performance income over a lifetime (not a starting salary):

.... $/yr × 40 yrs = $............................

3. Subtract minimum wage for a lifetime from a high-performance lifetime career income:

High-performance lifetime wage: $......................

Minus........................... Minimum wage for a lifetime

= $............................ Difference between the two salaries

If you decide that you'd like to pursue a high-performance career, you may ask yourself, "what am I currently worth in the workplace?" and using the 8 Cornerstones, determine which skills you already have and which ones you need to acquire in order to attain the career you want.

Me Inc Success Skills

The Me Inc career success skills have eight components: attitude, educational and career vision, self-management skills, fundamental skills, workplace skills, contacts, experience, and personal life.

The U.S. and Canadian governments have outlined these workplace competencies in detail (SCANS Workplace Competencies and Employability Skills 2000+). See pages 65 and 68, respectively.

ME INC AND THE 8 CORNERSTONES OF HIGH PERFORMANCE

01 ATTITUDE
02 EDUCATIONAL AND CAREER VISION
03 SELF-MANAGEMENT SKILLS
04 FUNDAMENTAL SKILLS
05 WORKPLACE SKILLS
06 CONTACTS
07 EXPERIENCE
08 PERSONAL LIFE

The 8 Cornerstones
of High Performance

1. Attitude
- positive outlook, motivation, initiative, work ethic, persistence, discipline, passion, coping with change and stress, willingness to learn, commitment to quality

2. Educational and Career Vision
- educational and career plans

3. Self-Management Skills
- time management, priority setting
- decision making

4. Fundamental Skills
- communication: written, verbal, listening skills
- creativity, critical thinking, problem-solving skills

5. Workplace Skills
- teamwork skills
- computer skills
- technology skills
- professional skills
- career competencies

6. Contacts
- networking, references
- mentors, industry contacts

7. Experience
- direct: part-time work, co-op/placement opportunities, volunteer work
- indirect: projects, unrelated work and volunteer experience

8. Personal Life
- family, friends
- health, lifestyle

Building Cornerstones

The 8 Cornerstones of Me Inc are the traits that will help you become a high performer and get a job with a high-performance salary.

1. Attitude
Positive outlook, motivation, initiative:

"Opportunityisnowhere."

Did you read that as "opportunity is nowhere" or "opportunity is now here"? It's the old "is the glass half empty or half full" question. Many employers say that the number one trait they look for is a positive attitude.

Work ethic, persistence, discipline, passion: These are arguably the most important workplace skills, next to a positive attitude. Having a good work ethic means being committed to doing whatever it takes to get a job done and seeing the job through to completion, regardless of the obstacles. Passionate people love what they do and bring enthusiasm and energy to their work.

Coping with stress and change: Employers love people who view problems as challenges and setbacks as opportunities for growth.

Willingness to learn: Look at new situations as learning opportunities, and be willing to learn a new skill if the situation requires it.

Commitment to quality: This is caring to do it right, from the smallest detail to the largest task. If you set employment standards for your college work, you'll develop a habit of producing quality work. Few people would give their boss a proposal that was thrown together at the last minute, so why not work on a paper as if you're preparing it for an employer?

2. Educational and Career Vision
If you've decided upon a career, you'll be able to

- gather educational and career information that's relevant to your profession,
- get a clear picture of how your education will lead to a concrete job,
- discover the skills you'll need to be successful in college and in the workplace, and
- make a clear educational and career plan and follow it.

If you don't know which career you want to pursue, that's entirely fine; you can focus on developing the employment skills that apply to all careers. Whenever you are ready to make your decision, you'll have the other essential employment skills in place.

3. Self-Management Skills
Time management, priority setting, decision making: Self-management ties in closely with work ethic and discipline and is a distinguishing characteristic of high achievers. Good self-managers know what needs to be done and manage their time so that it gets done on schedule. These kinds of people must be hard to find—the most common professional development seminar delivered around the world is on time management.

4. Fundamental Skills

Communication skills: Good written, verbal, listening, and presentation skills are essential to most professions and are highly valued by employers.

Creativity, critical thinking, problem-solving skills: It's important to be able to think critically, evaluate situations, collect information, and produce solutions independently.

5. Workplace Skills

Teamwork skills: A vital aspect of any job is the ability to work well in a group and deal effectively with all personality types. Leadership skills are also a part of group dynamics.

Computer skills, technology skills: It's a rare job that doesn't involve at least some computer work. You can greatly enhance your skill portfolio by learning as many different software programs and operating systems as you can. Many job candidates are selected because of their computer skills.

Professional skills, career competencies: These are the career-specific skills you'll need for your chosen profession. If you haven't yet decided which career is for you, you can concentrate on developing the other employment skills that are universal to all careers.

6. Contacts

Networking, references, mentors, industry contacts: It's been said that 85% of all jobs aren't advertised, so it's the people with the right contacts who are often successful in getting these jobs. The old saying "It's not what you know; it's who you know" has more than a measure of truth to it.

Creating contacts within your industry can start now. Networking could involve your classmates, your faculty members and any contacts they may have, your career resource center, professional associations, conferences and events, and informational interviews with professionals within your industry.

7. Experience

Direct and indirect experience: Because employers want someone with experience, your work history should contain as much relevant experience as possible. To maximize your value in the workplace, try to get as much direct experience as you can, whether through a co-op program or volunteer or part-time work in your field. If your program doesn't include a co-op component, volunteering is an ideal way to gain experience. You could find out which events or conferences are being held within your chosen field and volunteer your time at as many of them as you can. You could also approach a company you'd like to work for and offer your services. A part-time job and/or volunteer work can often be that "foot in the door" that leads to a full-time job.

8. Personal Life

It's important to maintain balance in your life and make sure you leave time for family, friends, and a healthy lifestyle.

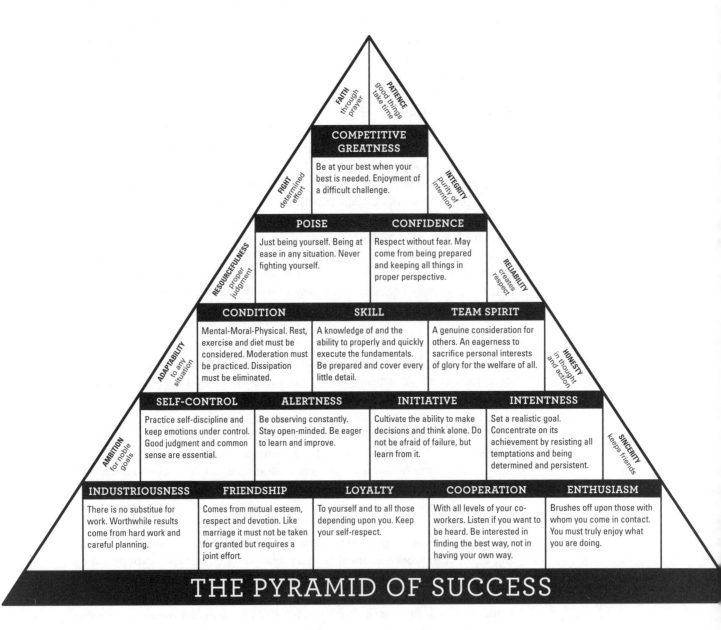

THE PYRAMID OF SUCCESS

"Success is peace of mind which is a direct result of self-satisfaction in knowing you did your best to become the best that you are capable of becoming."

– *John R. Wooden, Head Basketball Coach, Emeritus, UCLA*

Building Strengths

Exercise

1.3

During the interview process, most companies won't ask about your GPA but will instead focus on the strengths you bring to the workplace. So it makes sense to develop your Me Inc skills and to work on your academic requirements with a goal of developing the qualities that employers are looking for.

Pyramid of Success

a. Using the Pyramid of Success, choose five of the 25 strengths you feel you're good at and list them below.

1...

2...

3...

4...

5...

b. Get into a small group and share your list with the other group members. How many people in your group chose the same strengths you did? Which single quality do you think is the core strength of college and workplace success?

....

....

c. Choose one of the 25 strengths that you'd like to improve upon and suggest a few ways you could develop this trait.

Trait:...

1...

2...

3...

We can't stress enough that your Me Inc career success skills will set you apart in a competitive workplace. Your degree, associate degree, or diploma is essential in acquiring the educational background you'll need; your Me Inc skills will increase your value in the workplace and will set you apart as a motivated self-starter, a continuous learner, a problem solver with a solid work ethic, and a positive employee who works well with others.

Exercise

1.4

Employability Skills

Choose at least eight employability competencies outlined in the SCANS Workplace Competencies (page 65) or the Employability Skills 2000+ (page 68), and using the 8 Cornerstones of High Performance, place each competency under the most relevant category listed below. Make sure you find at least one competency for each Cornerstone.

1. Attitude

....

....

2. Educational and Career Vision

....

....

3. Self-Management Skills

....

....

4. Fundamental Skills

....

....

5. Workplace Skills

....

....

6. Contacts

....

....

7. Experience

....

....

8. Personal Life

....

....

Building Relationships

Interpersonal relationships are key to high performance. Not only will you be more successful if you have a solid support system behind you, but the social bonds you form will help you enjoy the journey more along the way.

From a career perspective, while your faculty members are fundamental to your education and career, your classmates are arguably the most important group of people related to your career—years from now, it may well be a fellow graduate who leads you to a key job connection or opportunity.

While it is commonly known that relationships are the foundation for adapting to new environments such as college, it's of particular interest to note that they're also the foundation for developing new habits such as your Me Inc high-performance skills. Bestselling author Alan Deutschman determined this when researching why only 10% of heart bypass patients change their lifestyle after surgery. Studies show that without proper support, bypass patients revert to unhealthy diet and living habits; however, when connected with a strong peer support group, 99% maintain new, healthy lifestyle changes for good.[1] Deutschman concluded that there are three keys to lasting behavioral change:[2]

1. Relate
People are more likely to make significant change when they form new, emotional relationships within a group that inspires and sustains hope.

2. Reframe
These new relationships help people learn new ways of thinking about their situation and their lives. Part of this reframing at the college level is the change in perception of study skills. In the context of a high-performance career, you can learn to perceive these skills as lifelong self-management skills that will see you through your college years and throughout your career.

3. Repeat
Within this new group, people learn, practice, and master the new habits they'll require to be successful. Within your college community, use your classmates and faculty to encourage you to keep using these new skills until the skills become habit and automatic. As Deutschman says, change requires training and lots of repetition over time.

Exercise

1.5

Their names:

....

....

....

....

....

....

....

....

....

....

....

....

....

....

....

Getting to Know You! Class Icebreaker

Interview 15 classmates.

The best thing to do in my hometown is ...

My favorite holiday/trip was ...

My favorite leisure activity is ...

The best part of high school was ...

The most frustrating thing about
high school was ...

My most memorable arts, sport, or
leisure experience was ...

If money were no object and I could do
anything I wanted, I would ...

Two things I'm looking forward to this
year are ...

Two questions I have about my transition
to college are ...

With regard to academic self-management,
my strengths and my weaknesses are ...

At school, two motivators and two
de-motivators are ...

My greatest expertise is ...

My future ideal job would be ...

My biggest concern about college is ...

During my college experience,
I hope to get involved in ...

Their responses:

....

....

....

....

....

....

....

....

....

....

....

....

....

....

....

**High-Performance
Change**

It takes a significant commitment to move your skills to a high-performance level. The motivation to persist can come from focusing on your long-term career goal and from perceiving your education as professional development for your career.

To make the behavioral changes required to become a high performer, it may help to break down the process into seven stages.

7 Stages of High-
Performance Change

Exercise

1.6

1. Review past academic performance.

Using *Exercise 1.6: Academic Self-Management Questionnaire*, take a look at your previous schoolwork habits and identify any areas that could use improvement.

Academic Self-Management Questionnaire

Rate yourself in the following areas. Mark an "x" in the circle that best reflects your past behavior and/or perceptions, and a checkmark (✓) in the circle that best represents where you'd like to be this semester.

Time management
- ○ 7 Highly effective
- ○ 6
- ○ 5
- ○ 4
- ○ 3
- ○ 2
- ○ 1 Ineffective

Quality of notes
- ○ 7 Detailed and complete
- ○ 6
- ○ 5
- ○ 4
- ○ 3
- ○ 2
- ○ 1 Incomplete

Study system/skills
- ○ 7 Well-developed
- ○ 6
- ○ 5
- ○ 4
- ○ 3
- ○ 2
- ○ 1 Weak

Binder/organization
- ○ 7 Highly organized
- ○ 6
- ○ 5
- ○ 4
- ○ 3
- ○ 2
- ○ 1 Disorganized

Study environment
- ○ 7 High quality
- ○ 6
- ○ 5
- ○ 4
- ○ 3
- ○ 2
- ○ 1 Low quality

Commitment to education
- ○ 7 High
- ○ 6
- ○ 5
- ○ 4
- ○ 3
- ○ 2
- ○ 1 Low

Class attendance
- ○ 7 Never miss
- ○ 6 Rarely miss
- ○ 5 90%
- ○ 4 80%
- ○ 3 Inconsistent 70%
- ○ 2 Weak 50-60%
- ○ 1 Poor < 50%

Procrastination
- ○ 7 Never
- ○ 6
- ○ 5
- ○ 4
- ○ 3
- ○ 2
- ○ 1 Always

Contd→

Exercise

1.6

Contd

Career goals	Projected fall results:
○ 7 Well-defined	1. Midterm GPA or % ....
○ 6	2. First semester GPA or % ....
○ 5	3. What's your #1 concern this semester?
○ 4	
○ 3	....
○ 2	4. As a follow-up to this exercise, I'm going to:
○ 1 Unclear	....

Behavioral change is the key to improving your self-management skills
To bridge the gap between past behavior (x) and desired behavior (✓), you need to identify what changes you need to make and commit to making them happen. It usually takes 21 days to develop a new habit, so hang in there—things should get easier and become routine after you make it through the transition period.

2. Explore limiting beliefs.
Do you have any beliefs about yourself that limit your performance? If so, you can take this opportunity to make a fresh start and let go of old self-perceptions. For example, if you've always seen yourself as a procrastinator, you can start to make better use of your time and develop a positive image of yourself as an efficient time manager.

3. Identify positive and negative motivators.
What internal and external motivators can you identify that (1) hold you back and (2) inspire you to be successful? We've started you off with an example of each.

Negative Motivators	Positive Motivators
ANXIETY	A GOOD JOB

4. Identify high-performance techniques and systems.

Take note of the high-performance habits you currently employ. Then, using the areas of improvement that you identified in Exercise 1.6, research new techniques and systems outlined in the relevant chapters of *Making Your Mark*. In the spaces below, list the techniques you think may work for you.

....

....

....

For a collective look at the success skills in *Making Your Mark*, your class could complete *Exercise 1.7: Making Your Mark*.

Exercise

1.7

> **Making Your Mark**
>
> **Part 1—Career/college success skills task**
> 1. Take 25 minutes and speed-read *Making Your Mark*.
> 2. Choose what you think are the four most valuable points in the book, and be able to discuss why they are important to you.
> 3. Hold a small group discussion.
> 4. Survey says ... On the board, have the class summarize statistically the most important points in *Making Your Mark*.
>
> **Part 2—Assignment**
> For the next class, reread *Making Your Mark*, and identify the same or four different important ideas/techniques and explain why they are important to you.
>
> *Format:* One page, 300–500 words, word processed or handwritten.
> *Due:* Next class.
> *Grading:* Complete/incomplete.

5. Create new patterns and habits.

It takes 21–45 days to change or create a new behavior, so you'll need to stick with each new behavior for three to six weeks for it to become permanent. Identify a concrete plan of action for each new pattern and do something every day to practice it. Keep up with your plan until each behavior becomes a habit.

6. Evaluate short-term results.

Take note of your progress and see how well an organized system works for you. Reward yourself for your progress.

You can illustrate the benefits of having a systemized approach to your schoolwork by completing *Exercises 1.8.1 and 1.8.2: The 100 Test–Parts 1 and 2*.

Exercise
1.8.1

The 100 Test—Part 1

In 50 seconds, circle as many numbers as you can in sequence from 1 to 100.

42 34 14 58 93 13 41 81 53
62 74 97 57 21
2 98 90 73 1 37
46 70
94 10 65 49 5 69
30 6 78 29
50 18 61 77 17
54
38 22 25 9 45 85 33
82 86 26 89
66

27 11 39 7 56 12 8 24
55
63 87 83 47 67 92 48 52 80 16
64
35 3 15 91 44 60 20 84 96
19 31
95 43 23 72 28 4 40 36
51
75 71 79 59 32 68 76
99 88 100

Exercise

1.8.2

The 100 Test—Part 2

Draw a horizontal line through the center of the numbers, and connect the
+ symbols. Then draw a vertical line straight down through the center of the
numbers, and connect the ▲ symbols.

In 50 seconds, circle as many numbers as you can in sequence from 1 to
100. Start in the top left quadrant. You'll find the numbers, one at a time, in
subsequent adjoining quadrants.

▼

42   34   14   58   93   13   41   81   53
62   74   97   57   21
2   98   46   90   73   1   37
94   10   70   65   49   5   69
30   6   78   29
50   18   61   77   17
38   22   54   25   33
82   86   26   89   9   45   85
66

+   +

27   11   55   39   7   56   12   8   24
63   87   83   47   67   92   48   52   80   16
35   3   15   91   44   64   20   84   96
95   19   43   23   31   60   28
51   72   4   40   36
75   99   71   79   59   32   88   100   68   76

▲

Note the difference in your results when you have an organized system
and approach to your work.

7. Adopt a lifelong approach to academic and career success.

If you envision yourself as a professional-in-training while at college and as
a lifelong learner in the workplace, you'll find the motivation to make high-
performance behavior changes and adhere to them. To put a number on making
the most of your college experience, you might want to complete *Exercise 1.9:
Return on Investment (ROI)*.

Exercise

1.9

Your ROI—Return on Investment

Calculate the cost of your college education for one year, and then divide that by the total number of classes you have scheduled. This will give you the cost per class of your education.

Direct Costs

Tuition ....

Books ....

Computer Equipment ....

Accommodation ....

Food ....

Transportation ....

Telephone ....

Clothing ....

Entertainment ....

Subtotal $ .... A

Indirect Costs

Lost Wages .... B

Total Cost (A + B) $ ....

Cost per Class

Total Cost ÷ Total no. of classes $ ....

= the cost per class

When you see how much you're paying for each class, it might inspire you to both attend classes and make the most of class time. Maybe it helps to look at it this way: when you buy a movie ticket, you aren't likely to throw the ticket away and skip the movie. Hopefully you can apply the same kind of value to your classes and earn a high rate of return on your college investment.

The 2,000 Hour Commitment

Success takes time; it takes anywhere from 12 months to four years in an educational setting to develop entry-level professional skills. It's been said that it takes 2,000 hours of repetition/learning to reach a solid level of accomplishment in any given field. To illustrate this, the 2,000-hour figure is the equivalent of an intensive 12-month college program or a two-year associate degree or program, and is also the minimum number of hours of on-the-job work experience required to complete an apprenticeship program. Success won't happen overnight, but in the long run, your efforts will be worth the investment.

Exercise

1.10

The Signature Exercise

1. Put your pen in your non-dominant hand.
2. Write your signature and the phrase "High-Performance Career":

....

3. Show your results to two other people.
4. What negative things did you say to yourself as you were writing?

Notice what it's like to change behavior with regards to your comfort level, efficiency, feelings of self-doubt, and results. Did the other two people have similar reactions to yours? Note the commitment it takes to make a change in behavior.

How's it Going?

It's important that your instructors know how you're doing so they can identify any areas or ways they can offer support.

Exercise

1.11

How's It Going?

Feedback memo
Format: Memo to instructor (please include a follow-up phone number and email address).
Content: Provide a brief and honest written update on how you're doing in each area listed below (one paragraph per heading; rate each one on a scale of 1–10).
Grading: Complete/incomplete.

Memo topics:
1. Intro to college/college success course.
2. Academic program (or major).
3. College life (sports, leisure, residence, community).
4. Personal life (friends, family, health, part-time jobs).

Building Success Skills

The success skills outlined in this book are the foundation for Me Inc and the 8 Cornerstones of High Performance. They are designed to help you be more efficient in how you use your time and how you study and to help you get the best possible academic results. We hope they're helpful to you.

Those who continually look for ways to learn, develop, research, network, and enjoy generally have the smoothest and most successful career paths. All the best in yours.

1 Alan Deutschman, *Change or Die: The Three Keys to Change at Work and in Life* (New York: Harper Collins, 2007), p. 48
2 Deutschman, p. 14

02 TIMING IS EVERYTHING

Do your work. It's as simple as that. Complete assignments on time, study for your tests, and do your homework. That's the secret of time management—getting your work done. The difference between knowing about commitments and actually getting around to fulfilling them is the difference between a poor time manager and a good one. And a great time manager is someone who gets his or her work done early so they've got time to do a quality job.

We believe that if, at the very least, you keep up with your assigned work, you'll probably make it through college successfully. Why? It seems that once the work piles up and you get too far behind, it's almost impossible to catch up. In fact, unsuccessful students pinpoint falling behind as the largest contributing factor to their failure.

The advantages to staying ahead of your workload are many: you enjoy your work more, you learn more, you don't get stressed out, you have time for quality, you get better grades, and your overall college experience is more fulfilling. Many people use schedules to help them with their balancing act.

Staying on Top of It All

It may sound obvious, but keeping track of what you have to do ensures that you don't forget to study for a test or keep a commitment. We recommend using schedules to give you a visual picture of how much work is building up. This will help you spread out your workload so you'll be less likely to hit a crunch time and have to pull all-nighters to get everything done. Three different types of schedules will help you stay on top of it all.

Semester Schedules

A calendar that displays one semester at a time will allow you to keep track of important dates and deadlines. If you keep your semester schedule where you can see it, you'll always be aware of what's coming up so you can plan how and where to spend your time.

Weekly Schedules

A weekly schedule will give you a detailed picture of each week's activities. Start by filling in your "must do's"—classes, study hours—and then leisure time.

Regular study hours?!
Most students wouldn't dream of scheduling regular study periods. While we acknowledge that there are more exciting things to do than study, we can offer three reasons why you may consider giving it a try.

1. Practice makes perfect.

Think back to when you were first learning your multiplication tables. Your elementary school teacher probably had the whole class recite each times table until you had them memorized. Repetition and review are two core principles of learning; the more you practice, the faster and better you learn. Study periods give you the opportunity to look over your notes regularly so that studying for a test is a quick review, not a monumental task.

2. Get more done.

Most students limit their study time to completing homework assignments. We're not knocking that—it's certainly important to do your homework. But on a light homework day, you could get a lot more done. Let's say you've set aside two hours to study on a given evening, and your homework takes only 45 minutes. You could use the remaining hour and 15 minutes to work on a major report or to review the day's notes. Your workload will be lighter later in the semester, when you'll probably need and appreciate the extra time.

3. Become a more efficient learner.

It's been proven that if you study at the same time in the same place on regular days, you become conditioned to study. In other words, when you sit down at your desk and open your books, your brain knows what you're there for. You don't have to sit around for 20 minutes trying to get into the right frame of mind. It becomes automatic.

Be realistic

However you decide to schedule your time, be realistic about yourself. If you know you're not going to sit down for four hours every Tuesday night and study, don't schedule it. Far better to set aside two hours and follow through. And if you can't live without watching your favorite weekly sports telecast, don't try to make yourself study then. A schedule is effective only if it suits your individual personality.

Daily Schedules

A "to-do" list will remind you of what you have to do each day. Prioritize each item on your list, and label the most important items "A," the less important ones "B," and the least pressing items "C." Start with your A's so that you finish your most important tasks first, and then work through your B's and C's.

Mike's To-Do List: Wednesday

A Proofread essay before handing in
B Read Chpt. 4 of accounting text
A Study for mgt. test
C Call Jen
A Return library books

A Mgt. homework assignment
C Wash dishes
B Do laundry
A Call home
C Buy ink cartridge at bookstore
A Book racquetball court (1:45 p.m.)

Time Wise

Scheduling can help you manage your time, but there are other ways of getting the most out of a day. We've compiled a list of time-management techniques that have proven useful to other students.

1. Do it now.
It's a simple concept, but if you decide to tackle one of the items on your to-do list right now, your list will disappear before you know it.

2. Say no.
There's nothing more tempting than an invitation to go out with a group of friends, and sometimes you really need a break from your books. However, if you can put a higher priority on studying for a term test, for example, the results will be worth the effort. If you can't say no, see whether you can't force yourself to fit in your study period before you go out.

3. Use your class time well.
Attend. There's no real substitute for being there. Information is better retained if you hear it firsthand. When it's time to study for a test, you'll remember more than if you had copied someone's notes (and you'll be taking the chance that his or her notes are complete and easy to understand). Your study time should therefore be shorter and easier. *Listen carefully.* The more you absorb in class, the less you have to relearn on your own. *Take notes.* If you keep a good set of notes, studying for tests and exams will be easier.

4. Start projects as soon as they are assigned.
Many people have the best of intentions, but few ever follow through on this concept. It's probably one of the most important, though, since the reason for most D papers is the fact that they were written the night before they were due. Assignments always seem to pile up, and you may find that three or four major papers are due at the same time. A little work on a report every week will allow you time to add quality to your work.

5. Divide each task into small, manageable chunks.
When schoolwork piles up, it's often hard to know where to start. Sometimes it seems as if you'll never get everything done. Break each task into smaller parts and the work won't seem as overwhelming. For example, instead of facing a whole chapter of your business administration text, set a goal of reading eight pages.

6. Use small pockets of time well.
Many students feel it's not worth doing schoolwork during breaks between classes because they won't have time to finish it. If you've broken your homework and assignments into smaller chunks, though, you'll be able to complete one or two of them in that time. You may even find yourself with a free evening.

7. Use your best time well.
Some people are "morning" people, so they should do as much work as possible early in the day. Nighthawks are better to save their work until the evening, when they are most effective.

8. Don't put off until tomorrow what you can do today.
Before the day is over, do one more thing that you were saving for "tomorrow." In time, you'll find that you aren't procrastinating as much. Moreover, your workload will be lighter.

9. Turn off the television.
Friends reruns are a great way to relax, but when you add *The Young and the Restless, Wheel of Fortune,* and *Jerry Springer* to the list, you may look back at your day and wonder where it went. Unless it's a "can't miss" show, try to save television until you've finished your homework.

10. Try the 10-minute ticker.
If you've got a to-do on your list that you find particularly unpleasant, try working hard on it for 10 minutes. You may find you don't mind continuing beyond the 10 minutes; at the very least, you'll have more of it done.

11. Stop studying.
Some people get carried away with trying to do too much. Make sure that your studies don't take over your whole life. It's important to balance college work with a variety of leisure activities.

Exercise

2.1

Getting the Monkeys off Your Back

Most of us have trouble finding enough time for everything we have to do. Taking a look at how you spend your time may help you reevaluate which things are priorities and which ones you can spend less time on.

Below is a list of activities that ordinarily take up at least an hour a week; we've left space for to you to add your own ideas. Rank the items from 1–5 in order of importance to you, and assign each one a number that indicates how many hours per week you spend on that particular activity.

Ranking	No. of Hours		Ranking	No. of Hours	
....	....	Watching television	....	....	Studying
....	....	Doing laundry	....	....	Spending time with friends
....	....	Going places (transportation)	....	....	Being with family
....	....	Going online	....	....	Attending classes
....	....	Working	....	....	Doing schoolwork
....	....	Doing schoolwork	....	....	Socializing
....	....	Playing video games	....	....	Other

> **Take your time**
> Now that you have a clearer picture as to where your time goes every week, ask yourself how many of these activities will be valuable to you five years from now. In our experience, most of us rank family #1, friends #2, and education #3. If these are your priorities and/or if you see a discrepancy between what your priorities are and how you're spending your time, this exercise might help you reassess whether you use your time in a way that's consistent with what's important to you.

Students with Part-Time Jobs

Balancing school, homework, and your personal life takes careful time management. When you take on a part-time job as well, it can be a challenge not to burn out. If money isn't a survival issue, try to limit your work hours. It's tough to be effective at anything when you're exhausted. However, if your job is essential to your finances, you may want to consider the following.

1. Don't waste your time.
You probably won't have much free time, so it will be important to use every minute well. If you've got a free hour between classes, try to get as much homework done as possible. If you finish lunch early, you could catch up on a reading assignment.

2. Don't try to stick to a set schedule.
It might be more effective to keep a to-do list and then use each pocket of free time in your day to complete the items on your list, in order of priority.

3. Take care of yourself.
You can't afford to let yourself get run down, so eat well and try to get as much rest as you can.

Nontraditional Students

If you're a nontraditional student, you face an added number of concerns. Will I fit in? Am I too old? Will I remember how to take an exam? How will I handle school and a family?

What's important for you to remember is that you've developed time-management and organizational skills during your working years and while raising your family. These skills will help you manage your life during your college years. Faculty and administration are aware of your additional responsibilities and are supportive of the individual needs you may have.

Nontraditional students generally do well because they have a clear purpose for attending college—a change in career, for example—so they are motivated and committed to their studies. The downside to this is that they often strive for excellence and place yet another demand on themselves. Considering family, financial, and academic pressures, it's important to realize that you can't do it all. Sometimes it's OK to be satisfied with "good enough."

03 NOTETAKING

"Do I need to write this down?"

How many times have you asked yourself this question in the middle of a lecture? Deciding what's important enough to include in your notes and what's not can be difficult and frustrating. Teachers tell you that you shouldn't try to write down everything that's said in class, but you don't want to leave out important information. On top of that, it's often hard to keep up with the pace of the lecture, and key points can slide by before you get them down. The system of notetaking that we endorse helps to eliminate these difficulties by simplifying the process to a single question: Is this likely to be on a test or exam? In other words, you write down only the concepts and ideas you feel you will be tested on, in a format that simultaneously prepares your study notes. This system is called 4R and consists of good listening skills and selective notetaking skills.

Listen to This!

To be an effective notetaker, you have to be a good listener. It's tough to keep your mind from wandering during a class, but you'll save yourself a lot of aggravation if you can stay tuned in to the lecture. First of all, you won't miss the important stuff, so your notes should be complete. You won't have to spend time copying a classmate's notes to supplement your own. Second, studying for a test should be easier. When you really listen to a lesson, you'll be surprised at how much of it you remember when you go back to review your notes. You'll be refreshing your memory rather than looking at the material for the first time. We've got some tips on how to "LISTEN" to even the driest subject matter.

L – Lead

Keep yourself in the lead; prepare for your classes. *Prepare physically.* Be ready to write as soon as your professor starts talking. Often an outline of the lecture is given at the beginning of the class so you can make note of the key areas of importance. *Prepare mentally.* A few minutes spent preparing for class is time well spent. Skimming the next chapter of your text to become acquainted with new vocabulary and ideas will make the lecture easier to follow. This will help you decide what's important and what's filler. A quick glance at your notes from the previous class will refresh your memory and set the stage for the present class. This review is especially helpful for students who are having difficulty.

I – Ideas

If you try to write down everything that's said in a lecture, you end up listening word by word rather than listening for the meaning of what's being said. Instead, try to look for the main ideas and concepts that should be included in your notes.

S – Summarize

As you listen, try to summarize the lecture into key concepts and ideas. Your professor will indicate main ideas by using phrases such as "in conclusion …," "four reasons for …," and "the characteristics of …." When you hear these kinds of cue words, it's a good idea to include the information in your notes.

T – Talk

Take part in the class. Even if you don't like a particular subject, you might as well try to make the best of it. You've got to be there anyway, and you may find that you enjoy the class more if you take on an active role. Answering questions and offering relevant opinions can turn a class into an interesting discussion and help you resist daydreaming.

When you're having trouble grasping a particular concept, don't be afraid to ask for clarification. If you're afraid you'll look stupid, look at it this way: it's better than trying to teach yourself something you don't understand when you're studying for a test.

E – End

The last five minutes of the class are often a summary of the lecture. Use this time to fill in any holes in your notes rather than packing up your books so you can be the first one out of the classroom. The conclusion is a valuable part of the lesson.

N – Notes

Take good notes. Listening effectively is the first step of notetaking, but you'll retain as little as 20% of the lecture after only 24 hours unless you review. We've got some ideas on how to keep your notes to a minimum yet make sure they contain the maximum amount of information.

First Class Notes

Before we get into the specific details of notetaking, we'd like to make a case for getting off to a good start. The first class of each course lays the foundation for the rest of the semester, so it's important to be there. Course outlines are introduced, teacher expectations detailed, and grading systems explained. This groundwork will help you tailor your style of notetaking to your instructor's teaching style. Does your instructor lecture straight from the text? If so, you may simply have to highlight key passages of your textbook. Are the lecture notes a supplement to the text? Or does the professor not use a text? If this is the case, your notes will have to be much more detailed. Whatever your professor's style of lecturing, you'll need a notetaking style of your own.

Taking Notes in Class

The method of notetaking we recommend is the 4R method. It's a simple system that will save you an enormous amount of study time because the notes you take in class are your review notes. Before you begin, divide your page into two columns by drawing a vertical line on your page about 2½ inches (6 centimeters) from the left edge. Some bookstores carry 4R notepaper (also called Cornell paper) to save you the bother of drawing the lines. The 4 R's are explained below.

Recall/Summary	Main Column
1. Record.	During the lecture, record in this column the most important facts and ideas presented.
2. Reduce.	As soon after the lecture as possible, review your notes to see whether they make logical sense, and then summarize (reduce) the facts into key words and phrases in the recall column. Write down questions you think you may be asked on an exam. These key words will act as test questions when you study. Note areas that need clarification.
3. Recall.	Cover the main column. Using only your cues and questions, see how much of the content you can recall aloud. Then uncover your notes to see how accurate you were. This procedure is extremely effective in transferring facts into your long-term memory. It's the same way actors learn their lines.
4. Review.	If you review your notes regularly, you'll retain most of the information. Studying for an exam will then be a review process, not a learning process.

The 4R system will definitely help you study more effectively, but what if you need help deciding what's important enough to write down? What if you can't keep up with your teacher? How can you best organize your notebooks?

Notetaking Tips

If you look at tests and exams as a summary of your courses and your notes as the answers to test and exam questions, you'll have an easier time pinpointing what you should include in your notes. Here are some other ideas.

1. Read/skim your text before class.
We've mentioned this briefly, but we'd like to emphasize three benefits:

a) When the lecture begins, you'll know which are the main areas of study and which are less important.
b) You'll be more familiar with the terminology/vocabulary.
c) The lecture will be reinforcement; you'll be getting your first review of the topic when everyone else will be hearing it for the first time.

2. Go early, stay late.
The first five minutes of a class are usually a summary of the previous class. Getting there early and setting up before your teacher begins will allow you several minutes to go over your notes.

You'll be ready to add anything you've missed. If your instructor gives an outline of the upcoming lesson, you'll be able to jot it down.

You can count on a busy end to the class. The last five minutes are either a summary of the lesson or are packed with everything your instructor couldn't fit into the first 45 minutes. If you put away your books early, you could be missing the most important part of the lecture.

3. Sit close to the teacher.

A correlation exists between grades and where you sit in the classroom. There are exceptions to the rule, of course, but generally, the closer to the front of the room a student sits, the higher the marks he or she earns. Why?

Sitting up front makes it easier to keep your attention on the lesson, as there are fewer distractions. It's easier to hear your professor. And it seems that students who sit near the instructor work harder.

4. Don't try to take down everything.

It's impossible, and you'll only get frustrated. Focus on the main points and any examples used to illustrate them. Important ideas are indicated by

a) time: the more time spent on an idea, the more important the idea.
b) blackboard/presentation screen: if it's written on the board or shown on a presentation screen, it's probably important.
c) videos, DVDs: if your teacher takes the time to show you a DVD on the subject, you'll know it's a significant area of study.
d) emphasis: if the concept is repeated many times, it's another indication of key material.
e) teacher: if your teacher looks at his or her notes carefully before making a point, it's likely to be important.
f) summary statements: they often contain the concept in capsule form.

5. Use abbrev.

Your own set of abbreviations and symbols will save you time in class. We have a list of examples, but we emphasize that whichever you use be familiar to you. It won't do you any good to make up a whole new system and then forget what the symbols mean when you go back to study your notes.

according	to acc to	important	NB or *
and	&	management	mgt
continued	contd	maximum	max
definition	def	number	#
department	dept	therefore	∴
each	ea	should be	s/b
equals	=	results in	→
example	eg	without	w/o
first	1st	versus	vs

6. Use lots of paper.

If you cram your notes together, you'll probably have a tough time deciphering them later on. Use lots of space and they'll be easier to study from. Don't squeeze diagrams or graphs into a one-inch square, and make sure you label them well so that you'll understand them when you have to study for a test.

Write on one side of the page only. This is not a waste of paper! Your notes will appear less crowded and will be easier to organize. The left (unused) side of the page can be used for integrating notes from the text, for filling in notes that you've missed, or for making study notes.

7. Leave spaces if you can't keep up.
If your professor is a speed demon, don't panic. Get down what you can, leave spaces, and listen carefully to the rest of the lecture. Immediately after the class, fill in the missing information; you should remember most of it. If you don't, borrow a friend's notes to get what you've missed. If you repeatedly have trouble following the lesson, make an appointment with your teacher to talk about possible solutions.

8. Use a separate binder for each subject.
Everyone has his or her own preference, but most top students prefer this note-keeping system. A small three-ring binder makes handouts easy to incorporate, and it's easy to insert notes in the right place if you've missed a class. Large binders designed for six subjects fill too quickly. Furthermore, you won't lose your notes for six subjects if you lose one binder.

9. Don't rewrite.
Rewriting your notes as a method of studying is not usually recommended. Reviewing your notes aloud is faster and more effective reinforcement.

10. Compare notes.
Sit down with two or three classmates, and exchange notes; you'll get a different perspective of what the most important course information is. Discussing why your peers took down certain points may help you see what should be included in your notes and what is unimportant.

Taking good notes is essential to your success. Your memory isn't reliable on its own. After only 24 hours, up to 80% of what you absorbed in a lecture is forgotten. Regular review, however, can reverse these numbers so that you retain at least 80% of the course material.

Exercise

3.1

Improve Your Notetaking Skills in One Hour

How different would your notes be if you knew that they were going to be passed around the class for everyone to look at?

In the student success workshops we run, we tell the students early in the day that their seminar notes will be circulated among the participants at the end of the workshop. All of the students improve their notetaking skills significantly. The reason they give for this improvement is that they don't want to be embarrassed in front of their peers. We point out to them that just by caring more and by deciding to do so, they take better notes—and when they combine that intent with the techniques outlined in this chapter, they can improve their notetaking skills even more significantly.

Taking Notes from Your Text

Reading some textbooks can be pretty boring. It's tough to keep your mind on the book, and many people find that when they've finished, they can't remember what they've just read.

We'd like to make your reading time a little easier and a lot more productive. We've got a couple of suggestions.

First of all, try not to get behind. Reading a chapter of your text may seem a great chore on a given evening, but the task takes on monumental proportions when you've got five chapters to plow through. And when a task feels too overwhelming, you may not bother doing it, yet teachers take many of their test and exam questions straight from the text. Even better, try to get ahead of the readings so that class time is a review of the material you've read. Short and frequent reading sessions are most effective; it's easier to absorb the material in shorter sittings.

The textbook notetaking system we advocate is called S4R, and it works along the same lines as the 4R system of classroom notetaking. It's based on the premise that most authors write in outline form so that each paragraph contains a main idea and supporting details. The idea is to look for key ideas that are likely to be test or exam questions, always keeping in mind that your notes will double as your study notes.

S – Survey

Leaf through the chapter, and skim the introduction, glossary, and summary; look at the review questions; and take note of the titles, subtitles, charts, graphs, and illustrations. These will give you a general idea of the chapter's content and will help you identify the main ideas being presented. The survey should take no more than five minutes.

R – Read

As you read the chapter, don't read word by word, sentence by sentence. Rather, skim through unnecessary details, and search only for the main ideas of the chapter. How do you identify them? Generally, they are definitions, words highlighted in bold or italics, and the key concepts you identified in your survey. Remember, you're looking for potential test questions.

R – wRite

Using 4R notepaper (see "Taking Notes in Class" on page 28), write down the important ideas in the main column, and then reduce them to key phrases in the recall/summary column. These phrases will be your review or study questions.

R – Recall

Take a minute to see how much of the content you remember by using your recall phrases as a prompt. Then look at the main column to see how accurate you were. If you go through this process aloud, you'll learn the material far more quickly than if you limit yourself to reading your notes over and over again. Rehearsing your notes aloud may seem far fetched to some, but we feel that the goal is to learn the material as quickly as you can so that you've got more time for more exciting things. Feeling a little awkward may be worth the end result.

R – Review

Pull out your study notes and review them on a regular basis. Learning is like preparing for a marathon. It takes lots of training. You wouldn't leave getting in shape for a 26-mile race until the night before; learning and studying require the same preparation.

So that's the S4R method of reading your textbooks. You don't waste time reading unnecessary details, and your study notes are prepared as you read. You focus on grasping only the key concepts, so you don't have to memorize the entire text. When you prepare for a test or exam, it's easy to zero in on what you really need to know. We think the benefits are worth the extra effort.

Guidelines for Marking Your Text

If you prefer to make notes directly in your text, make sure that you don't over-mark your book. Too much is worse than not enough—a cluttered book is difficult to read. There are two ways of marking your text: highlighting and making notes in the margin of the book. Here are some ideas on both systems.

Highlighting

If you like to use a highlighter, skim each paragraph before you put any marks on the page. Many times a sentence will seem to be important the first time through, but as you read on, you find either that it isn't as important as you originally thought or that the same point is made more clearly later on. Once a section is marked, you'll end up studying the information whether or not it's important because it is highlighted. However, if you highlight only 15–20% of your text, you'll save yourself rereading 80–85% of it at exam time.

Marginal notes

If you've chosen to make notes in the margin, use a consistent marking system so that your notes will have some meaning when you start your review. We have a few suggestions.

Underline: key phrases, main ideas
Indicate an important paragraph:]
Make notes in the margin. Some examples are noted below.

def	= definition
eg	= example
NB/ *	= important point
?	= unclear point
1, 2, 3	= items in a list

04 STUDY HINTS AND SHORTCUTS

First-year students have a lot of advice about studying thrown at them during the first few weeks of college. "You should study an hour on your own for every hour you spend in class." "Your study habits will have to be a lot different than they were in high school." "You'll have to put in time if you want to get anything out of this course."

Not only is this kind of advice intimidating, it doesn't tell you a lot. What exactly should you be doing during your study time? Does every course require an hour of studying for every classroom hour? And what if you sit down to "put in time" but find your mind always seems to wander?

Studying isn't as hard as you think. Sure, it takes time and effort, but if you follow a few proven study techniques, you can decrease the amount of time you spend at the books and increase the amount you learn. In fact, we are convinced that success skills play as important a role in college success as does intelligence.

17 Ways to Study Smarter

1. Attend classes.

Don't make the mistake of cutting classes and trying to teach yourself from the text or from a friend's notes. Make it easy on yourself—your teacher has already done that work for you. Since it's the information your professor thinks is important that will appear on a test or exam, it makes sense to go to class and find out what that is. You'll then be spending your study time reviewing what you need to know, not teaching yourself what you hope you need to know.

Pay special attention to the last five weeks of the semester. It's been said that 50% of a course's work takes place in the last third of the term.

2. Know your instructor.

Take time to learn what's needed to get through each subject. Study the syllabus (course outline), and refer to it periodically to make sure you're on track. Find out your instructor's testing format, grading/marking system, and expectations. You'll be able to tailor your work to meet his or her requirements.

3. Schedule regular study periods.

If you don't set aside a specific time to review, chances are you won't review. The most effective way to learn anything is to rehearse it regularly. Whether you are practicing the piano or sports or reviewing your notes, you are learning through the principle of repetition.

4. Be realistic.

When you make up your schedule, decide how much time you really want to study, and divide that time among your courses. It's better to spend half an hour on each subject than to plan one hour for each one and not follow through.

5. Establish a regular study area.

When you study in the same place every time, you become conditioned to study there. Your mind will automatically kick into gear, even when you don't feel like studying.

A regular study area also gives you a permanent place to keep your notes, texts, pens, and other supplies. You won't waste 10 minutes each day collecting the materials you need— they'll already be there.

6. Study short and often.

Your brain takes in information faster and retains it better if you don't try to overload it. Four short study periods a week are more effective than two long ones for two reasons: (1) frequent repetition is the key to building your memory and (2) if you leave a longer time between study periods, you may forget a good portion of the material you studied.

7. Start study sessions on time.

It sounds like a small detail, but it's amazing how quickly those 10-minute delays add up. Train yourself to use every minute of your scheduled time.

8. Study when you are wide awake.

The majority of people work most efficiently during daylight hours. In most cases, one hour during the day is worth 1½ hours at night. That's one of the reasons we encourage you to use the hours between classes and other small pockets of time during the day wisely.

Decide what your best time is and try to schedule your study time accordingly. You accomplish more when you are alert. If you find yourself nodding off, give in to it. It's better to wake up early to finish the last hour of homework than try to get through everything when you can't think straight.

9. Set a specific goal for each subject you study.

You'll accomplish more—faster—if you set a specific goal for each study session. Let's say you've set aside 30 minutes to read your accounting text. If you start reading without a particular purpose, you may get only nine pages read. But if you set a goal of 15 pages in that time period, you'll probably finish all 15.

So instead of sitting down to "study computer math," you could decide to answer the review questions at the end of the chapter. Or instead of "studying marketing," you could set a goal of completing the outline for your marketing paper.

One last thing: don't worry if you don't reach your set goal within the allotted time. Either reschedule the task into your next study period or go back to it later that evening if you have enough time.

10. Start assignments as soon as they are given.

If you do nothing else from this chapter, do this. A little work on an assignment each week will allow you time to give attention to its quality. Your workload will be spread out, so you'll avoid a logjam near the end of the semester. If your assignment is due near exam time, as many major papers are, you'll avoid using valuable study time to complete your paper.

11. Study your most difficult subjects first.

You're most alert when you first sit down to study, so you'll be in the best shape to tackle the tough stuff. You'll also feel better getting the worst out of the way, and you won't be tempted to spend all of your time on easier or favorite subjects.

12. Review your notes regularly.

Taking good notes is the first step; reviewing them regularly is the second. As we keep saying, the best way to learn anything is to review the information (aloud, if you will) often. When the time comes to be tested, you'll only have to review. You won't have to learn it all.

We've outlined a review schedule below. You may want to add to it if you're having difficulty with a particular subject.

1st review: same day (reduce to key words)
2nd review: later the same week
3rd review: one week later
4th review: two to three weeks later
5th review: monthly

You'll retain up to 80% of the course material in your long-term memory.

13. Take regular breaks.
The general rule of thumb is a 10-minute break for every 50 minutes you work. Don't study through your breaks—they rejuvenate you for your next hour of studying.

14. Vary your work.
Try to give yourself some variety in the type of studying you are doing. For example, if you tried to read textbooks for three hours, you'd not only get bored, you'd have trouble processing the information. Instead, alternate reading, taking notes, doing homework, and writing papers. It's important to vary the subjects you're working on, too. A change is as good as a rest.

15. Problem solve.
For courses that require you to solve problems, such as math, physics, chemistry, and statistics, spend a good portion of your study time working on problems. Much of the testing content will be presented in problem form, so you'll be preparing yourself for exam time. If you get stuck on a homework question, don't spend the rest of the night on it. Go on to the next question, and ask for help the next day.

16. Reward yourself.
When you complete a study goal, give yourself a reward. It doesn't have to be anything elaborate—a magazine, snack, movie, or TV show. The reward system gives you an incentive to reach your goals and a pat on the back for achieving them.

17. Keep on top of it.
Letting work pile up can leave you with an overwhelming task. It's easy to feel that you'll never get it all done. If you find yourself falling behind, you may need to work on your success skills. Maybe you need to improve your time management. Or maybe the solution is as simple as cutting down on your social life. Identify the problem as soon as you can, and don't let it become unmanageable.

I Can't Concentrate

If you're the kind of person who sits down to study and ends up daydreaming about where you're going Saturday night, you might find the following concentration techniques helpful.

Clear your mind
When thoughts of "things to do" jump into your head, free your mind by dealing with them right away. If a particular job won't take long to do, you may want to get it out of the way right now. An alternative is to jot it down on your to-do list for later.

Focus!
Mental discipline works. If you tell yourself, "I'm going to study hard for this exam, and when I'm finished, I can daydream all I want," you'll find that you're better able to keep your mind on your work. It's been proven that you can train yourself to develop your concentration abilities.

Don't worry about it
Try not to spend your study time worrying about personal problems. It's easier to say than do, but try to put your problems aside while you're working. If they continue to dominate your thoughts, don't try to study—you simply won't be able to get anything done. Give them your full attention, and try to come up with solutions. If things get too bad, talk to a friend or teacher, or make an appointment to see a college counselor.

Switch subjects frequently
If your attention span is short and you are easily bored, switch the subjects you are studying frequently. Variety helps ward off boredom.

Do not disturb
Shut yourself away from noise and distractions. Don't give yourself a chance to be diverted. Television, phone calls (have someone take a message), family commotion, and nearby conversations will all hamper your concentration.

Zzzzzzzzzzzzzz
Lack of sleep destroys your ability to concentrate. Most people need between seven and nine hours of sleep every night. Your body functions best on a schedule; constant changes in your sleep habits are both physically and mentally disruptive.

Don't Forget to Remember

If you weren't lucky enough to be born with a photographic memory, you can improve your ability to retain information by following some of the memory techniques outlined below.

Be selective
Pare down the information to the key facts—you'll have less to remember. With practice, you'll learn to take down only what is important.

Repeat after me

Repetition is the key to a good memory. The fastest and surest way to transfer information from your short-term to your long-term memory is to rehearse or review often, preferably aloud. If you've ever had to recite a poem or book passage in front of an audience, you probably practiced aloud until you had it memorized. It's an effective way to learn.

Intend to remember

If you decide to remember the material, you will. If this sounds too simplistic, think about how a waiter makes a conscious decision to remember your order. The waiter remembers it because he or she has to. By the same token, if you make a commitment to remember your course material, you will.

Like what you learn

When you're interested in something, the details are easier to remember. A die-hard baseball fan, for example, can remember ERAs and batting averages without any difficulty. The same person may have a terrible time remembering scientific formulas, especially if he or she doesn't like the subject. If you can turn the material into a personal interest, it will be easier to retain. It may help to see the course as part of a long-term career goal.

Find meaning in it

Information that is meaningful is learned more quickly and remembered longer. When you are trying to learn something that you don't understand or is unrelated to anything you know, it's very difficult to retain. If you can associate it with something you're familiar with, you'll have a much easier time committing it to memory.

Get organized

Sometimes categorizing the material will make it more meaningful. You might have a hard time remembering your shopping list in the first formation, but when you rearrange the items into categories, it suddenly becomes a much easier task.

pens	laundry detergent	paper
shampoo	ramen noodles	peanut butter
bread	binders	paper towels

School	**Food**	**Household**
pens	ramen noodles	laundry detergent
paper	peanut butter	shampoo
binders	bread	paper towels

Find a pattern

Learning miscellaneous items or lists can be difficult unless you find a pattern to help you remember them. If you had to remember the number 16,385, for example, you could break it into two patterns:

1–3–5 (odd)
6–8 (even)

Make it rhyme

"In 1492, Columbus sailed the ocean blue."

"Thirty days have September, April, June, and November."

Few of us ever forget rhymes. You might want to try your hand at rhyme to help you remember small details or major concepts.

Use acronyms

SCUBA (Self-Contained Underwater Breathing Apparatus) is a well-known acronym. HOMES reminds you of the names of the Great Lakes (Huron, Ontario, Michigan, Erie, Superior).

Both rhymes and acronyms can be effective memory tools, but don't spend too much time trying to devise them.

Assign a number

If you were trying to remember the types of joints in the human body, it would help to jog your memory if you knew that there were five kinds. In a test situation, if you could remember only four types but knew that there were five, you would be more likely to come up with the fifth type.

Come to your senses

Hearing and sight play important roles in memory work. That's one of the reasons we promote rehearsing (hearing) notes. Imagine how hard it would be for a comic to learn a routine without practicing it aloud. Rehearsing also makes it easier to detect any errors or weak areas and moves facts from your short-term to your long-term memory faster.

Sight (visualizing) gives your mind a picture to associate with the information. Visualizing actual events, diagrams and illustrations, or important points marked with colored pens will paint you a mental picture that will help imprint the material into your memory.

Keep it short

Study periods can last up to 50 minutes if you're reviewing, taking notes, or doing homework, but for straight memory work, they shouldn't be longer than 20–30 minutes without a break.

Concentrate on the middle

The material you review at the beginning and end of your study sessions will be remembered best, so you won't need to spend as much time on it as you will the middle content.

Sleep on it

If you review your notes right before you go to bed (assuming you're still alert), your brain will continue to process the information all night and reinforce it as you sleep. It's an easy way to learn!

Read Between the Lines

As much as 85% of your college work involves reading. It follows, then, that the better you read, the more success you'll have in your courses. If you find reading an effort, don't worry—comprehension and speed can be improved with practice. Daily practice is most effective, and only 15 minutes a day will do it.

Choose something you find easy to comprehend, and read it at your best speed. Take note of how much material you got through after 15 minutes, and take a second to make sure you absorbed the important details (if you didn't, you were probably reading too quickly). For the first two weeks, continue to read the same type of material, and see how many more pages you can read in each 15-minute period. Push yourself a little, but don't compromise on comprehension. Keep a record of your progress.

Gradually increase the difficulty of your reading material, and follow the same procedure as above. In six weeks or so, you'll have greatly improved your reading ability.

Studying Isn't Everything

There's more to college success than studying. Your relationship with your teachers, your attitude, and your involvement in college life can all make your college years more productive and enjoyable.

Your Faculty

It's important to get along with your faculty. Often a dislike for a teacher results in a dislike for the subject, which in turn can result in a lower grade. The question isn't "Do I like this teacher?" but rather "How much can I learn from this teacher?" A good relationship with your faculty will maximize your learning experience.

The Right Approach

Learning and studying require dedication and commitment. So does playing varsity basketball. The connection? They're both hard work, as are most things, but it's how you approach them that makes them enjoyable or a drag. The same intensity for basketball can be put into your schoolwork, with similar results: personal satisfaction from your efforts.

It's easy to maintain a positive attitude about your studies if you surround yourself with people who want to get the most out of their college education. Instead of putting continual pressure on you to go out for a good time, they'll have more interest in getting their homework done and will encourage you to do the same.

College Life

College doesn't begin and end in the classroom. Getting involved in college life will give you a well-rounded education. Movie nights, intramurals, public lectures, student council, interest clubs, the library, and the athletic complex will add to your enjoyment of your college years.

05 PAPERS, REPORTS, AND ASSIGNMENTS

It's essential to develop good writing skills since most jobs will require you to turn out effective business communications. Your papers and assignments will give you a foundation for writing business memos, letters, and proposals.

Keep it simple

Many people try to add quality to their papers by using big words and complicated sentence structure. However, these often have the opposite effect. A concise writing style is easier to read and understand. Simple words are generally most effective. A thesaurus is a great writing aid and will help you select the most precise words for your thoughts.

Sentences cluttered with unnecessary words are also confusing to the reader. "I myself" is commonly used but is incorrect; "I" alone is all you need. Other phrases such as "due to the fact that" ("because" will do), "until such time as" ("until"), and "at this point in time" ("now") make sentences long and unclear.

Each sentence should include one main idea only, and a paragraph should consist of a group of sentences that relate to one common theme.

Do spelling and grammar count?

Nothing puts your credibility in question more than errors in spelling and grammar. Proper punctuation, spelling, and sentence structure are essential to your assignment. If your writing skills are weak, you may want to inquire about extra help or peer tutoring. At the very least, be sure to proofread your papers or have someone else read them over before you hand them in; you don't want your teacher focusing on correcting your spelling rather than giving full attention to the content of your report.

Writing Your Paper or Report

Before you begin working on your paper, be sure you understand the precise requirements of the assignment. It's essential that you follow your instructor's directions. Too often students write about their topics from the perspective of the source rather than shaping the material to address their professor's expectations.

The Right Topic

The first step in writing a good paper is choosing a feasible topic. Poor papers are generally the result of weak topics. Make sure there is enough research and information available to support the topic you've selected.

Putting It All Together

When you've gathered your research and information, make an outline for your report so that you present the information in logical progression. Write your first draft from your outline, and take a break (preferably for a few days). Then go back and review it for accuracy, content, style, spelling, and punctuation. You'll be better able to edit your work when you've been away from it for a while.

Begin and End Well

The introduction is one of the most important parts of your paper. First impressions count, and you want the person grading your report to consider it an A paper right off the bat. The introduction should give the background of the paper and generate interest in the subject. It should state what the paper will cover: the theme, purpose, and scope.

The conclusion is a summary of the main purpose of the paper and can include a personal evaluation of the subject and any recommendations you may have.

Essays vs. Reports

The format of an essay differs from that of a business report. An essay supports a thesis statement through a clear presentation of evidence. Each main point should be presented in its own paragraph in logical sequence. Prove statements with facts, research, and illustrations. On the other hand, a report requires an organized presentation of information.

You Can Judge a Book by Its Cover

It's important to spend time on the presentation of your assignment. A professional-looking report will often receive a better grade than one that was put together with little thought. Your report folder, title page, table of contents, bibliography, appendixes, and word-processed pages will all enhance your assignment and reflect positively on your grade.

References

There are several formats for citing sources. Your course may use APA or MLA, for example, or may have its own set of report-writing guidelines. Check with your teacher to make sure you use the required format.

Bibliography

As with footnotes, a bibliography can be laid out in a number of ways, so make sure you use the format your instructor is looking for. Keep a list of the resources you use as you conduct your research so that you don't forget to include any. Interviews and electronic sources should also be listed in your bibliography.

Plagiarism

Most people think that plagiarizing is copying word for word from a source. However, it also includes taking the thoughts and ideas of others and presenting them as your own. Paraphrasing a source is also classified as plagiarism. Avoid any problems by footnoting properly. Check your college's policy on plagiarism; there are usually severe penalties for those found guilty of an infraction.

06 HOW TO STUDY FOR EXAMS

So much emphasis is placed on the importance of exams that just hearing the word can make people nervous. We hope that the following information will make your life during exam week a little easier.

There's no doubt about it—preparing for exams takes a lot of work. We would like to offer our thoughts on how to make your study time easier, more productive, and hopefully shorter.

Getting Started

The first step in preparing for exams is learning the exam format, topics, and weighting with regard to your final grade. These details will help you determine what and how long to study. If your instructors won't tell you what's on the exam, pay special attention to their particular areas of interest and to topics that were emphasized during the semester. If the exam format is objective, you'll need to spend more time learning specific details, while essay exams focus more heavily on general concepts and ideas.

If you used the 4R and S4R systems of notetaking, you'll already have a set of study questions and answers. You won't have to spend time making up study notes. However, if you didn't use these notetaking systems, we've got some suggestions on how to spend the minimum amount of time studying to gain the maximum results.

Exercise
6.1

How to Prepare a Study Checklist

Probably the best way to start is to prepare a study checklist, similar to a table of contents. Using your notes, text, and syllabus, make an outline of the major topics that were covered in the course. Divide each heading into subtopics. For example, a management student might identify "decision making" as a major topic and a subtopic as "the seven steps of decision making."

The checklist should take no more than 15 minutes to prepare and will provide you with an overview of the entire course. You'll then know what you have to study, and you'll have a good idea how long it will take to cover all the material.

Summary Sheets

When you've finished your checklist, you'll have a skeleton outline of your course. The next step is to make up a detailed summary sheet for each major topic.

Exercise
6.2

How to Make a Summary Sheet

The general idea is to take each subtopic from your checklist and write down a key word or phrase that will help you remember the entire concept. It is especially helpful to phrase it in question form. For example, a question from the management student's summary sheet might be "What are the seven steps in decision making?" Information to be included on a summary sheet may include definitions, vocabulary, calculations, any points emphasized in class, or a list of items from a paragraph in your text (lists make perfect test questions—beware!).

After you have identified the key word or phrase for a subtopic, write down all of the relevant information you feel you would need to know for an exam. Do this with each point on your checklist. When you've finished, you'll have a complete set of study notes. You won't have to look at your lecture notes or textbook again. You'll have a neat summary of the entire course in the form of potential exam questions.

A word of caution: write only enough to jog your memory. Don't fall into the trap of rewriting your entire notes. You'll only be wasting time on a lot of details you don't need to know.

How to Use Your Summary Sheets

The most effective way to use your summary notes is to ask yourself the questions you've prepared aloud and to answer them aloud as often as you can.

Rehearsing the answers is the fastest way to learn; reading them over and over is the slowest. Give rehearsing a chance—we're convinced that it won't take you long to see what a difference it makes. You'll learn the material faster. You'll also find out which areas are easy for you and which need a lot of work so that you can allocate your time accordingly.

Practice Tests

Practice tests are extremely effective study aids. They work best when you test yourself a few times during the semester, but you'll still benefit if you wait until exam time.

The advantages of practice tests are many: (1) you'll increase the number of questions on the exam that are familiar to you, (2) you'll give your study sessions a focus, so you'll be less likely to waste time, (3) the best preparation for an exam is to practice exactly what you'll be doing when you actually write it, and (4) you'll eliminate the stress of exam time because you'll have answered so many practice questions that the real thing will be old hat to you.

Exercise

6.3

How to Set up Practice Tests

What questions would you ask on a test if you were a teacher?

Keeping this question in mind, set up a practice test by using your study questions, old exams, and textbook review questions. If possible, use the same test format that your professor uses (if that happens to be multiple choice, here's where old exams are particularly helpful—check your college library).

When you sit down to take the test, simulate test conditions as closely as you can. Whatever you do, don't look at your notes until you've finished the test. You won't get a true picture of what you know and where you need to spend more time.

You can grade your test by comparing your answers to your notes. If you spot an area that needs work, set up the next test to concentrate on that particular topic. Don't spend too much time on the areas you know well.

Studying for Science and Math Tests

When you're studying for a math or science exam, start by compiling a summary page of formulas and definitions. Make details of the steps to follow when solving each particular type of problem, and solve sample questions and problems for each concept.

A Grab Bag of Exam Study Tips

1. Be prepared.
The most important factor in exam success is preparation. Bar none. No matter how many helpful hints you employ, nothing works as well as making sure you've studied enough.

2. Do your homework.
Often an exam question will parallel a homework assignment. Doing your homework regularly will give you practice where you need it.

3. Review regularly.
If you spend a few minutes each week reviewing your notes, your final studying will be a review, not an attempt to learn the entire term's work.

4. Study your weakest subjects first.
Why? You'll be fresher and therefore better able to deal with difficult areas, and you'll have more time to deal with any problems that arise.

5. Ask for help.
If you're having trouble with a particular subject, don't be afraid to ask for help. Your teacher and fellow students will be glad to give you a hand. Remember, too, that most colleges have peer tutoring programs. See your student services department for details.

However, don't leave asking for help until the last minute. It's impossible to teach a semester of accounting in a week. If you find that you're struggling with something early on, get help immediately.

6. Understand vs. memorize.
You may pass your exams if you memorize the material, but you'll improve your grades considerably if you understand what it is you're memorizing. You'll also find the material easier to remember.

7. Look at old exams.
Some teachers file copies of past exam papers in the library. They can be useful study tools, as long as you don't limit your studying to them.

8. Attend end-of-semester classes.
A lot of valuable information is outlined in the last few classes of the semester. Points of misunderstanding can be cleared up, exam format explained, and potential exam questions given.

9. Review in a group.
But make sure the review doesn't take the place of your own study time. Brainstorm possible test questions with your classmates, compare notes, and test one another on the material.

10. Don't study too long.
A 10-hour study marathon will only wear you out. You'll learn more if your study periods are short, frequent, and include regular breaks.

11. Eat well and get a good night's sleep.
Take care of yourself during exam week—you're going through a lot of stress. Make sure you hold up well.

Last-Minute Cramming

Although we've included this section on cramming, we don't advise it for one important reason.

Cramming isn't learning. Most of what you cram will be forgotten in one or two days. In other words, if you cram for a term test, the information won't be there for the final exam. That's why we believe so strongly in regular review.

Assuming you have no other choice, here are the four steps of cramming.

1. **Be selective.** Don't try to learn everything—it's virtually impossible. Go to your syllabus (course outline), text, and notes, and choose a few of the course highlights. Learn these topics as best you can. You're taking a chance on the content of the exam, but you really don't have any other choice. If you try to learn a little about a lot, chances are pretty good you won't remember much of anything.
2. **Question and answer.** Turn the information you are about to learn into a series of exam questions and answers, and start drilling yourself. Take a five-minute break every half hour.
3. **Rehearse.** Rehearsing the answers aloud is the most effective way of remembering course material. Study as long as you are able, and stop when it seems nothing is sinking in anymore.
4. **Do your best.** Try to relax, and go out and do the best you can.

How to Write an Exam
Give Yourself a
Good Start

The morning of an exam can be fairly stressful. Try to ease the tension by giving yourself a good start to the day.

Get a good night's sleep if you can, and make sure you have a trusty alarm clock. Nothing is worse than writing your exam in a hurried panic because you were late.

Be certain of your exam time and place. Arrive early enough to get settled and arrange your workspace but not too early; it's not a good idea to get into a last-minute discussion with frantic classmates. Your friends' worries will only add to your own. And last, we don't recommend you sit near your friends. It's too distracting. You'll be tempted to see whether you're ahead of or behind their pace and to make periodic checks as to how they're doing. You'll also be more likely to leave early if you see them walking out ahead of time.

Hints for Objective
Exams

Objective exams may include multiple-choice, true-false, short-answer, or matching questions. Nearly all of the information is supplied on the exam itself. In most cases, your job is to recognize the correct answer.

Many students don't study as hard for objective exams, but we encourage you to prepare as well for them as for any other exam. In fact, they are often more difficult than essay exams because there is a definite right or wrong answer. Either you know the correct answer or you don't.

Multiple-choice

Here are some hints to help you with multiple-choice exams.

1. Try to answer the question yourself before looking at the answers given.
2. Answer the questions you know first. Mark the ones you're not sure of, and go back to them.
3. Your first instinct is usually correct; don't change your answers unless you are sure you made a mistake.
4. Take questions at face value—don't get caught up looking for tricks. There probably aren't any.
5. Watch the meaning of sentences containing double negatives. Cross out both negatives, and then answer the question.

If you're having trouble:

6. Rephrase the question in your own words.
7. Underline key words. This can help untangle complicated questions.
8. Look for answers in other test questions.
9. Cross out the answers you know are incorrect, and select your answer from the remaining options.
10. Never leave a question unanswered unless there is a penalty for an incorrect answer. In that case, answer only if you can narrow your choices down to two.

Take a guess

No matter how much you study, you're bound to come across at least one question that will have you completely stumped. But even guessing is a science. Here's how to make your best guess:

1. If two answers are similar, choose one of them.
2. If two answers have similar words (perpetrate, perpetuate), choose one of them.
3. If two answers have opposite meanings, choose one of them.
4. Choose the longest answer.
5. If none of the above works for you, choose (b). Studies prove that (b) is the correct answer 40% of the time, (c) is right 30% of the time, (a) 20% of the time, and (d) only 10% of the time.

True-false questions

Since true-false questions are usually worth only one point, don't spend too much time on any one.

1. There are generally more true than false answers.
2. Look for qualifiers (all, most, sometimes, rarely). The answer will depend on the qualifier, and more often than not, questions containing qualifiers are true.
3. However, answers that have "always" or "never" in them are usually false since nothing (with the exception of some math and science questions) is true or false 100% of the time.

Short-answer questions

This is the only kind of objective question that relies on recall and usually requires a short description or definition.

1. Look for grammatical hints. For example, a sentence that begins with "An" indicates that the word starts with a vowel.
2. Use the best word or phrase you can think of.

Matching questions

Take a brief overview of the question before you start, as there are not always an equal number of items to match. Start with the easiest match, and cross out each answer as you use it to minimize the confusion of the question layout.

Hints for Open-Book Exams

These are often the most difficult exams because your teacher expects you to answer every question well.

1. Write all formulas, definitions, etc., on a separate sheet of paper for easy referral.
2. Prepare your notes for quick reference. Make a table of contents, number your pages, and tab important pages.

Hints for Science and Math Questions

1. Translate problems into English to help you understand what is being asked. For example, the formula for calculating interest, $I = P \times R/100 \times T$, would be translated as "Interest equals principal times the rate as a percentage times the time period."
2. Determine the unknown.
3. Determine the known quantities.
4. Write out the formula.
5. Show all your work. Don't skip steps, even if they seem trivial to you. Your teacher needs to see the logic of your answer and may give partial credit for each step of the solution.
6. Check for a logical answer. Make sure that what you have calculated makes sense.
7. Check to see whether you used all of the data supplied. It isn't often that data is given and not used.
8. Proofread your exam. Check the steps of each problem.

Hints for Essay Exams

1. **Read the entire exam first**. Roughly estimate the time allowed for each question according to the point value.
2. **Keep the grader happy**. Make your exam easy to read. Use pen, double-space your answer, and write legibly on one side of the page. You don't want your teacher's first glance at your paper to put him or her into a negative frame of mind.
3. **Answer the easiest question first**. This is a good way to build your confidence. Moreover, a strong first answer will help persuade your professor that you've prepared well for this exam.
4. **Read the directions carefully,** and do precisely what the question asks you to do. If you are asked to compare two theories, you'll lose points if you explain them, because you haven't answered the question.

A word of caution: one of the most common errors in writing essay exams involves questions with more than one part. If the question reads "Answer one of the following," don't waste valuable time answering all four parts. Conversely, if it reads "Answer all four parts," make sure you don't do only three. There is nothing more frustrating than knowing the material but losing points because you didn't follow the directions.

5. **Plan your answer.** Make a mini-outline, including all of the main points you want to cover. Your outline could be as simple as jotting down points as they occur to you and then numbering them in the order you want to use them.

   An outline will allow you to answer the question faster, and you'll be less likely to leave out an important fact. If you run out of time, your teacher will be able to see what you intended to write about and may give you partial credit.

6. **Get right to the point.** Don't waste time with an introduction. Make your opening statement forceful, and make sure it states exactly what you are going to talk about.

   Use your strongest points first to make an immediate impact. You want to convince your professor right off the bat that your answer is worth a high grade.

7. **Keep to the point.** Write only what is relevant to the question. Remember, grading an essay question is subjective. If the person grading your paper has to wade through pages of filler to find a few good points, he or she may get annoyed and not grade you as highly as if you used the same points in an organized, compact answer. Most teachers have at least 200 papers to get through and will look favorably on an exam that is easy to grade. The quality of your answer does not depend on the quantity of words you use.

8. **Don't forget to include the basics.** You may think that some things are too elementary to put down, but these may be the very things your professors are looking for. They can't assume that you know something you didn't write down, and you may be losing easy marks.

9. **Make clear your understanding of the material.** Illustrate your answers with examples and diagrams; your teacher is looking for more than memory work.

10. **Keep your eye on the time.** Make sure you're not spending too much time on one answer at the expense of the others.

11. **Always write something.** Even if you have no idea how to answer a question, try to relate the answer to other course material, another exam answer, or your general knowledge. At worst, you'll get a few points for your effort.

12. **What's the hurry?** Don't try to race through the exam. There aren't any marks for finishing first, so you might as well use the time allotted to perfect your paper.

13. **Proofread your paper.** Have you answered all parts of the question? Make any spelling and grammar corrections, and add any important points you've missed. Pick up as many extra points as you can.

14. **If you run out of time,** jot down the last few ideas in point form. Your teacher will be able to see where you were going with your answer, especially if you used an outline before you began.

15. **Don't rehash the exam with your classmates afterward.** If you forgot to include something or misinterpreted a question, there's nothing you can do about it now. You'll need all of your energy to concentrate on your next exam, so leave this one behind.

Read the Directions

You'll come across some of these words when you're writing your exams. Look them over so that you'll understand exactly what each question is asking you to do.

Analyze	Examine in detail. Involves judgment.
Compare	Show similarities and differences.
Contrast	Show differences.
Define	Explain the meaning in a short answer.
Describe	Tell all you know; include as many details as you can.
Discuss	Write everything you know in a logical progression.
Evaluate	Examine the positive and negative aspects; draw a conclusion.
Illustrate	Use specific examples and details.
Justify	Give reasons to support a position.
Outline	Using the main ideas, give an overview.
Prove	Use facts and evidence to support a position.
Summarize	Give the main ideas in a short answer.

Relax!

The ABC's of Eliminating Exam Anxiety

It's easy to say but a lot more difficult to do when you've got your toughest exam to write and you don't feel you've studied enough.

A. **Think positively.** Thoughts such as "I haven't studied enough" and "I don't know the material" will only increase your anxiety level. Instead, try to feel good about what you do know. You hear it all the time, but a positive attitude goes a long way.

B. **Take a deep breath.** It really will help you calm down. Think of a reward that you'll give yourself when you're through—maybe lunch out or a movie with a friend.

C. **If you draw a blank, don't panic.** It happens all the time. Take a few minutes to sit back and wait for it to come back to you.

D. **Don't look around to see what your classmates are doing.** If you're having doubts about how well you're doing and you see someone who looks like they're acing the exam, it will only add to your anxiety.

E. **Prepare well for your exams.** People who know the material rarely get nervous. Review regularly, and give yourself practice tests.

F. **Keep things in perspective.** Although exams are important, they're not a matter of life or death. Years from now, nobody will ask you what grades you received on your exams. They lose significance over time.

07 MANAGING COLLEGE LIFE

College Survival Skills

Starting college can be difficult. Moving to another city, living on your own, meeting new people, getting used to a new set of academic standards—all of these can present you with quite a challenge. But how you approach a given situation will determine whether it gets the better of you or whether you stay on top of it.

It's normal to feel down when things are difficult. That said, you still have to find a way to make it through the hard times. How do you cope when the going gets tough?

Try to do something constructive about your circumstances. People generally feel better when they feel like they're in control of a situation—rather than feeling like it's controlling them. If you're homesick, you could attend a social event to surround yourself with people and make new friends. If you're having a tough time academically, you might talk to a professor about doing an extra assignment to help you pass the course. If a relationship is ending, you could plan a weekend away with a friend.

If there's nothing immediate that you can do, decide how you'll better handle future situations, and try to learn from this experience. Your coping skills will improve with each new experience.

You still may find a situation getting the better of you. Here are some ways to help you develop your survival skills.

14 Ways to Cope With It All

1. Be resilient.
It's easier to deal with life if you can adapt to a variety of situations—for example, be hardworking and focused at exam time and carefree and relaxed when exams are over.

2. Be open minded.
It's easy to be critical of a situation or professor, especially if those around you are doing so. Don't let others be a negative influence on you. Keep an open mind and come to your own conclusions and you'll experience things in a more positive way.

3. Be yourself.
Other people may have an opinion on how you should handle things, but you have to do what works for you. You know yourself best—have confidence in your ability to handle things in your own way and in your own time.

4. Keep laughing.

Keep things from getting too serious by hanging on to your sense of humor. Find ways to have fun, and plan time with uplifting friends—a good laugh will make you feel a lot better.

5. Meet new people.

One of the best antidotes for feeling down is to go out and meet new people or participate in new activities. You may find that despite your difficulties, there's still a lot out there to enjoy.

6. Don't sweat the small stuff.

A renowned cardiologist's philosophy for dealing with stress: (1) Don't sweat the small stuff. (2) It's all small stuff.

7. Use the five-year rule.

Ask yourself: "Five years from now, how important will this problem be?" Nine times out of 10, the answer is "Not very important." The five-year rule can keep you from blowing the situation out of proportion.

8. Talk to someone.

Don't bottle your problems up. Go to someone you trust, and get it off your chest. Sometimes just verbalizing the problem can help you to see it in a different light. If things get bad enough, visit your student services department, and set up an appointment with a counselor.

9. Make your escape.

Taking a break can do wonders for your frame of mind. Your escape doesn't have to be as elaborate as a vacation; a shopping trip, movie, or walk in the park can do the trick.

10. Let it out.

Release your frustration in a productive way; a hard game of racquetball, for example, can help ease your tension.

11. Forget about it.

Sometimes you've just got to say, "This isn't important enough to give my time to" and move on from whatever's got you down.

12. Do something nice.

If you find you're thinking about your own worries too much, focus on someone else who's dealing with a tough situation. You'll get a good feeling from doing something nice for him or her, and you'll forget about your own troubles.

13. Do one thing at a time.

If your workload seems overwhelming, don't get discouraged. Take the most important task that's haunting you, and start on it. Accomplishing even one of your "to do's" can make you feel like you're back in control.

14. Give yourself a break.
Some people create stress by setting standards that are too high to reach. Don't try to be perfect—sometimes you'll have to be satisfied with "good enough."

Money Worries

One of the hardest things you'll do while you're in college is budget your money. When you receive your student loan and you're suddenly "rich," it can be tempting to run out and celebrate with a shopping spree.

Keep a budget so you'll have enough money at the end of the semester. Set a realistic amount for spending money, and stick to it. Spending too much with too little thought is where most students run into trouble. If you see that you are going to run short, you have several options.

A part-time job can bridge the financial gap. Your college's placement office can help you with your job search. You may be eligible for a work-study program (see your student services department). The financial aid office offers grant and scholarship programs and can determine your eligibility for student loans.

In the meantime, we have several ideas to help you stretch your dollars.

Don't carry around a lot of cash. People generally spend as much as they have with them. If you don't have it, you won't spend it.

Put away your credit card. It's easy to overspend when using a credit card because you don't feel like you're actually paying for the merchandise. It's also easy to forget you've spent the money until the bills come in.

Find affordable rent. If you're living off campus, figure out how much rent you can afford, and stick to it. You don't want to have all of your money tied up in housing.

Think again. If you're dying to buy a new CD or pair of jeans, give it some more thought. Often the item won't be as important in a day or two.

Wait until it's on sale. You may save a bundle if you're willing to wait a while.

Schoolwork Worries

If you don't do as well as you expected on your first few tests and assignments, don't despair. It takes time to become familiar with your professors' expectations and standards.

It's also common to periodically feel snowed under by your workload. Good time-management and success skills will help you deal with your anxiety. Whatever you do, don't give up, and don't spend all of your waking hours working. Long work sessions aren't as productive as short ones, and you'll only wear yourself out. Start with one job, and take it one step at a time.

If it all gets to be too much for you, talk to your teacher(s) to find out where the problem is. Together you can work out a solution.

College Services

Your college has a number of support services to help you make it through. *Exercise 7.1: Student Life Survey* will help you identify any further information you would like regarding these services and will help your faculty know what information you would like them to provide.

Academic Support
- Library, labs
- Peer tutoring program
- Faculty/staff
- Student services
- Registrar's office

College Support
- Career placement office
- Counseling, health services
- Financial aid, housing
- Student association
- Resident directors, assistants

Exercise

7.1

Student Life Survey

Name:...

Please circle the appropriate number.

Rate your awareness and understanding of:	No understanding					Very high understanding		For further information, check here and rank in order of priority

A. Nonacademic Support Systems

1. Career Placement Office	1	2	3	4	5	6	7	....
2. Student Financial Aid, Grants, Bursaries	1	2	3	4	5	6	7	....
3. Counseling/Guidance	1	2	3	4	5	6	7	....
4. Day Care	1	2	3	4	5	6	7	....
5. Housing	1	2	3	4	5	6	7	....
6. Athletic Complex Facilities and Services	1	2	3	4	5	6	7	....
7. Athletics/Intramurals	1	2	3	4	5	6	7	....
8. Student Association	1	2	3	4	5	6	7	....

B. Academic Support Systems

9. Faculty Advising/Office Hours	1	2	3	4	5	6	7	....
10. Peer Tutoring	1	2	3	4	5	6	7	....
11. Computer Resources	1	2	3	4	5	6	7	....
12. Student Service Counseling	1	2	3	4	5	6	7	....
13. Library Services	1	2	3	4	5	6	7	....
14. Grading System for Each Course/Subject	1	2	3	4	5	6	7	....
15. GPA/Program Grading Criteria	1	2	3	4	5	6	7	....

C. Career Information

16. Job Market Opportunities	1	2	3	4	5	6	7	....
17. Professional Competencies/Skills Required	1	2	3	4	5	6	7	....
18. Part-Time Job Opportunities	1	2	3	4	5	6	7	....

D. Program Guidelines/Policies

19. Attendance	1	2	3	4	5	6	7	....
20. Assignment Criteria (format, lateness)	1	2	3	4	5	6	7	....
21. Plagiarism	1	2	3	4	5	6	7	....
22. Field Work/Co-op/Clinical Practice	1	2	3	4	5	6	7	....

23. What further information would you like on college services and/or resources?

College Friends

Making new friends isn't always easy. Some of us meet people more easily than others, but it still takes an effort to form new friendships.

There are two things above all else that will help you make new friends. The first is to simply start a conversation. You have to take the initiative and approach the people you'd like to get to know. Those who sit back and wait for others to come to them may wait a long time.

The second is to be a good listener. People who have a genuine interest in others never seem to lack friends.

It's important to spend time with your friends. Your college experience will be richer for it; some of your best memories of college will be of class parties, intramurals, or student activity nights with your classmates.

College is an opportunity to make a fresh start, an opportunity to pursue the goals that are important to you. We wish you all the best in your journey.

08 Resources

SCANS Workplace Competencies (U.S.)

The workplace know-how identified by SCANS (U.S. Secretary of Labor) is made up of five competencies and a three-part foundation of skills and personal qualities that are needed for solid job performance.

Five Competencies

Resources: Identifies, organizes, plans, and allocates resources

A. Time: selects goal-relevant activities, ranks them, allocates time, and prepares and follows schedules

B. Money: uses or prepares budgets, makes forecasts, keeps records, and makes adjustments to meet objectives

C. Material and Facilities: acquires, stores, allocates, and uses materials or space efficiently

D. Human Resources: assesses skills and distributes work accordingly, evaluates performance and provides feedback

Interpersonal: Works with others

A. Participates as a Member of a Team: contributes to group effort
B. Teaches Others New Skills
C. Serves Clients/Customers: works to satisfy customers' expectations
D. Exercises Leadership: communicates ideas to justify position, persuades and convinces others, responsibly challenges existing procedures and policies
E. Negotiates: works toward agreements involving exchange of resources, resolves divergent interests
F. Works with Diversity: works well with men and women from diverse backgrounds

Information: Acquires and uses information

A. Acquires and Evaluates Information
B. Organizes and Maintains Information
C. Interprets and Communicates Information
D. Uses Computers to Process Information

Systems: Understands complex interrelationships

A. Understands Systems: knows how social, organizational, and technological systems work and operates effectively with them
B. Monitors and Corrects Performance: distinguishes trends, predicts impacts on system operations, diagnoses deviations in systems' performance, and corrects malfunctions
C. Improves or Designs Systems: suggests modifications to existing systems and develops new or alternative systems to improve performance

Technology: Works with a variety of technologies

A. Selects Technology: chooses procedures, tools, or equipment, including computers and related technologies
B. Applies Technology to Task: understands overall intent and proper procedures for setup and operation of equipment
C. Maintains and Troubleshoots Equipment: prevents, identifies, or solves problems re: equipment, including computers and other technologies

Three-Part Foundation

Basic Skills: Reads, writes, performs arithmetic and mathematical operations, listens, and speaks

A. Reading: locates, understands, and interprets written information in prose and in documents such as manuals, graphs and schedules
B. Writing: communicates thoughts, ideas, information, and messages in writing and creates documents such as letters, directions, manuals, reports, graphs, and flow charts
C. Arithmetic/Mathematics: performs basic computations and approaches practical problems by choosing appropriately from a variety of mathematical techniques
D. Listening: receives, attends to, interprets, and responds to verbal messages and other cues
E. Speaking: organizes ideas and communicates orally

**Thinking Skills: Thinks creatively, makes decisions,
solves problems, visualizes, knows how to learn, and reasons**

A. Creative Thinking: generates new ideas
B. Decision Making: specifies goals and constraints, generates alternatives, considers risks, and evaluates and chooses best alternative
C. Problem Solving: recognizes problems and devises and implements plan of action
D. Seeing Things in the Mind's Eye: organizes and processes symbols, pictures, graphs, objects, and other information
E. Knowing How to Learn: uses efficient learning techniques to acquire and apply new knowledge and skills
F. Reasoning: discovers a rule or principle underlying the relationship between two or more objects and applies it when solving a problem

**Personal Qualities: Displays responsibility, self-esteem,
sociability, self-management, and integrity and honesty**

A. Responsibility: exerts a high level of effort and perseveres toward goal attainment
B. Self-Esteem: believes in own self-worth and maintains a positive view of self
C. Sociability: demonstrates understanding, friendliness, adaptability, empathy, and politeness in group settings
D. Self-Management: assesses self accurately, sets personal goals, monitors progress, and exhibits self-control
E. Integrity/Honesty: chooses ethical courses of action

![Employability Skills 2000+ logo bar]

Employability Skills 2000+ (Canada)

The skills you need to enter, stay in, and progress in the world of work — whether you work on your own or as a part of a team.

Fundamental Skills
The skills needed as a base for further development.

You will be better prepared to progress in the world of work when you can:

Communicate
- read and understand information presented in a variety of forms (e.g., words, graphs, charts, diagrams)
- write and speak so others pay attention and understand
- listen and ask questions to understand and appreciate the points of view of others
- share information using a range of information and communications technologies (e.g., voice, e-mail, computers)
- use relevant scientific, technological, and mathematical knowledge and skills to explain or clarify ideas

Manage Information
- locate, gather, and organize information using appropriate technology and information systems
- access, analyze, and apply knowledge and skills from various disciplines (e.g., the arts, languages, science, technology, mathematics, social sciences, and the humanities)

Use Numbers
- decide what needs to be measured or calculated
- observe and record data using appropriate methods, tools, and technology
- make estimates and verify calculations

Think and Solve Problems
- assess situations and identify problems
- seek different points of view and evaluate them based on facts
- recognize the human, interpersonal, technical, scientific, and mathematical dimensions of a problem
- identify the root cause of a problem
- be creative and innovative in exploring possible solutions
- readily use science, technology, and mathematics as ways to think, gain and share knowledge, solve problems, and make decisions
- evaluate solutions to make recommendations or decisions
- implement solutions
- check to see whether a solution works and act on opportunities for improvement

Personal-Management Skills
The personal skills, attitudes, and behaviours that drive one's potential for growth.

You will be able to offer yourself greater possibilities for achievement when you can:

Demonstrate Positive Attitude and Behaviours
- feel good about yourself and be confident
- deal with people, problems, and situations with honesty, integrity, and personal ethics
- recognize your own and other people's good efforts
- take care of your personal health
- show interest, initiative, and effort

Be Responsible
- set goals and priorities, balancing work and personal life

The Conference Board of Canada
255 Smyth Road, Ottawa
ON K1H 8M7 Canada
T. 613.526.3280
F. 613.526.4857
www.conferenceboard.ca

- plan and manage time, money, and other resources to achieve goals
- assess, weigh, and manage risk
- be accountable for your actions and the actions of your group
- be socially responsible and contribute to your community

Be Adaptable

- work independently or as a part of a team
- carry out multiple tasks or projects
- be innovative and resourceful: identify and suggest alternative ways to achieve goals and get the job done
- be open and respond constructively to change
- learn from your mistakes and accept feedback
- cope with uncertainty

Learn Continuously

- be willing to continuously learn and grow
- assess personal strengths and areas for development
- set your own learning goals
- identify and access learning sources and opportunities
- plan for and achieve your learning goals

Work Safely

- be aware of personal and group health and safety practices and procedures and act in accordance with these

Teamwork Skills

The skills and attributes needed to contribute productively.

You will be better prepared to add value to the outcomes of a task, project, or team when you can:

Work with Others

- understand and work within the dynamics of a group
- ensure that a team's purpose and objectives are clear
- be flexible: respect and be open to and supportive of the thoughts, opinions, and contributions of others in a group
- recognize and respect people's diversity, individual differences, and perspectives
- accept and provide feedback in a constructive and considerate manner
- contribute to a team by sharing information and expertise
- lead or support when appropriate and motivate a group for high performance
- understand the role of conflict in a group to reach solutions
- manage and resolve conflict when appropriate

Participate in Projects and Tasks

- plan, design, or carry out a project or task from start to finish with well-defined objectives and outcomes
- develop a plan, seek feedback, and test, revise, and implement
- work to agreed quality standards and specifications
- select and use appropriate tools and technology for a task or project
- adapt to changing requirements and information
- continuously monitor the success of a project or task and identify ways to improve

About LDF Publishing Inc.

LDF Publishing Inc. has been assisting colleges with student success and retention ideas since 1992. *Making Your Mark* has sold more than one million copies and is used in more than 1,500 educational institutions across North America. Its strengths are its light and friendly writing style, its comprehensive coverage of essential material, and its cost. We've priced the book so that any college can afford to implement a retention strategy.

Lisa Fraser, author of *Making Your Mark*, also coauthored Cornerstone, the Canadian edition of a student success textbook for Prentice Hall Canada Inc. She has worked as an educational proposal writer, securing funding and grants for college projects, and has taught developmental education classes.

Don Fraser is one of North America's leading authorities on student success and retention. He has been a professor at Durham College for the past 30 years. He codesigned and implemented Durham's student success program 18 years ago and has been working in this area since that time. Don has done a great deal of research on student success and retention and received a NISOD award for this work. He has developed a retention model—"The Right Start to College"—that has been adopted by many colleges and universities across North America. Don was a member of the Ontario government's task force on student retention.

Products:

Making Your Mark, ISBN 978-0-9735298-3-8
Making Your Mark in the OHL, ISBN 0-9696427-7-6
Comment réussir dans ses études, ISBN 0-9735298-0-6

Faculty Development Seminars:

"*Making Your Mark:* Educational/Career Vision, College and Career Success Skills, Relationship Building"
"Student Motivation and High-Performance Change from Day 1 to Graduation"
"Staff/Faculty Retention Training"
"Key Performance Indicators (KPI) Retention Consulting"

About Our Products and Services

Making Your Mark is the foundation of our retention program. We've found that incorporating the book into a first-year orientation seminar produces dramatic retention results. Seminar outlines are available from our website www.makingyourmark.com.

"*Making Your Mark:* The Right Start to College" workshop has been delivered at the 1998–2007 National Conference on Student Retention, the 1999 World Congress of Colleges and Polytechnic, the 2002, 2003 and 2007 ACCC Annual Conference, the 2003, 2007 and 2009 Career College Association Convention, the 2005 and 2009 Student Engagement Conference, the Starlink Professional Development Network, the March 2009 Webinar for Innovative Educators, and at individual colleges to more than 17,000 college staff members. For more information or for help in developing your retention program, please contact Don Fraser at 1.877.492.6845 or 416.484.8118 or by email at info@makingyourmark.com.